Your life in the world is your story.
Write well. Edit often.

~ Anonymous

Also, by Leonard Neufeldt

Nearness
(Silver Bow Publishing, 2020)
Figures in Time
(Moonstone Press, 2020)
Painting Over Sketches of Anatolia
(Signature Editions, 2015)
How to Beat the Heat in Bodrum
(Alfred Gustav Press, 2010)
The Coat is Thin
(Cascadia Publishing House, 2008)
Before We Were the Land's
(Horsdal & Schubert, 2002) Heritage Award.
Car Failure North of Nîmes
(Black Moss Press, 1994)
Yarrow
(Black Moss Press, 1993)
Journal Volume 4, The Writings of Henry D. Thoreau
(Princeton Univ. Press, 1992)
Raspberrying
(Black Moss Press, 1991) Lambert Prize shortlist.
The Economist: Henry Thoreau and Enterprise
(Oxford Univ. Press, 1989)
The House of Emerson
(Univ. of Nebraska Press, 1982)
Awarded "1983 Best Academic Book," (national).
Christian Gauss Prize, Phi Beta Kappa Society shortlist.
A Way of Walking
(Univ. of New Brunswick Press Fiddlehead Series, 1972)

Find
What Isn't Missing

by

Leonard Neufeldt

720 Sixth St., Box # 5
New Westminster, BC
V3L 3C5 CANADA

Title: FIND WHAT ISN'T MISSING
Author: Leonard Neufeldt
Cover Design: "Masked Enigma" painting by Candice James
Layout and Editing: Candice James
© 2021 Silver Bow Publishing

ISBN 978177403 143-8(softcover)
ISBN 978177403 144-5(e-book)

Library and Archives Canada Cataloguing in Publication

Title: Find what isn't missing / by Leonard Neufeldt.
Other titles: Find what is not missing
Names: Neufeldt, Leonard, author.
Description: Poems.
Identifiers: Canadiana (print) 20210106360 | Canadiana (ebook) 20210106379 | ISBN 9781774031438
   (softcover) | ISBN 9781774031445 (EPUB)
Classification: LCC PS8577.E758 F56 2021 | DDC C811/.54—dc23

For Di Brandt, Marty Gervais, Neil Myers
and David Zieroth, magnanimous companions
who put me on the path and kept me there

Acknowledgements

My gratitude to editors of literary publications in which some of these poems appeared:

Alfred Gustav Press Chapbook Series 16 (December 2016): "Find What Isn't Missing"

Antigonish Review: "The Dutch Immigrant's Daughter"

Bellingham Review: "Alzheimer's Resource Finder"

Blue Lyra Review: Canto 18 of "Cantos on Time and Distance"

Borderlands and Crossroads (anthology):   "Addendum Filed with the Medical History"

Cede Poetry: "Homecoming"

Dalhousie Review: "Life Stories"

December: "Hymnal with Pressed Flowers"

Event: "In Response to Questions"

Hologram for PK Page (anthology):   "Covent Garden"

Moonstone Press: "The Clarity of Mystery; The Mystery of Clarity"; "Emmanuel Lévinás and the Unconditional"; The Farm Was for Tax Purposes"

NonBinary Review: Foreword and Cantos 1-5 of "Cantos on Time and Distance"

Prism international: "A Journal on Expatriates"

Queens Quarterly: "All She Wanted Was to Move to the City"; "Litany for Alice Munro"

Struggle for Freedom (anthology):   "The Procession in Soweto"

Rhubarb: "Housekeeping"

Voicing Suicide (anthology):   "Grace Holding Its Breath"; Canto 15 of "Cantos on Time and Distance"

Contents

CANTOS ON TIME AND DISTANCE

"We were still standing by the sea's new day
like travelers pondering the road ahead
who send their souls on while their bones delay"

~ Dante Alighieri, *The Purgatorio*, Canto II
(John Ciardi Translation)

Cantos on Time and Distance

Foreword

On a day a continent away
a kind of blackened violet
demanding full presence, the turquoise gulf
mirroring meteor flares bent by swells
and the impossible distance they feel
from Yucatán light no longer there

the endless roar of silence
and on the sky's far wall the large
round dusty blindness of the sun
and only raptors and scavengers
at their last meal to see it.
The earth plea-bargaining

**

the finer expression of birds, the light
changing the sea as squall lines and thin
shivers of rainbows pass through

I. The Searching Grounds

Canto 1

Lord of words tasted ages ago
under the iridescent heavens by those
wiser than assurances they wrote down
to hold a universe in place

Dante, exiled for refusing
to separate the passionate from the divine
and a world from hell and heaven,
dreamt in Ravenna of how earth and sun
and stars flew into the void
to their appointed position, keeping
their distance, keeping God's double measures,
how hell and paradise completed them

and how the king of time forbade
Virgil to leave the gates of hell because
the law that reaches past moon
and stars to a pilgrim's cantos cannot bless
the greatest poem of them all.
Domine, non sum dignus
but the pilgrim's guide must have known
Virgil too was worthy, and not only he,
for the uphill syncope
through hell with paradise on its mind

Canto 2

An epic distance of loss and gain
between its twinned supernovas,
which once flared the farthest ends
of what we see and know
and whose dying light still reaches us

with what comes after, so much happening
to confirm there is no time without
distance or distance free of time:
impossible as a star's birth without
the reach of a nebula or the start
of a new galaxy, terribly alone,
bereft of mass or light beyond itself,
still-born in the orphaned void

Canto 3

"More light," Goethe beseeched his last day.
The pilgrim knows that spires of form
must learn to live in the fitful here and now
and not where desire separates us
from ourselves and seeds that separation
with words desperate to unhinge themselves
from *now*, to rip away its cusp,
collapse it into moments of inmost swirl
seeking centre and circumference, yet holding
to a maybe *nowhere*, rush and pauses
its margin, the outer *nowhere* far too fast
for the inner maybe *maybe now*,
that possible flash of *what is*
in the maelstrom's creations
left to their unforgiving isolation,
fleeting an invisible trace
like some god particle already gone

Canto 4

Unlike the pilgrim's uphill miles,
his moments, ordinary or not,
still his searching ground
outside the gates of hell, staying in time,
his guide long gone, refusing to go farther.

No need to let the meridian's sides know
a hawk is riding the sky's poverty
past the sun, or that this shape out of reach
will not leave him although he's leaving
where he's been, the season getting shorter

Canto 5

After time has nibbled away the pilgrim's bones
and dust and the galaxies' fiery work,
all the years, forbidden to talk about themselves,
will shrink into a single separate
now and die, the end no longer a fine art,
and with the suddenness of a first flash
of day will body forth again
and bend with every new appearance
of near and far, feeding an old hunger
anew into what will be

II. Trying to Stay Ahead of the Past

Canto 6

So much too distal to know, to understand,
although for Homer distance was
the homelessness of the forever
Odyssean blue and time
was a faithful reaching back
of story-telling like the presbyopic editors
of Genesis, closer to Babylon
than Elohim's formless, empty world
or seas and gardens yet to be

Descendants well ahead of the past
continued where they were,
the holy land too far away
for a reunion of strangers
or for Eden's tropic flowers
and ancient hanging gardens
to burst into blooms fevered red,
almost close enough to reach

Canto 7

*Shoplifting from the long-ago
to set tables today or to say everything
is merely a matter of exchange will not feed
India's hungry*: Dr. Sharma, professor
of philosophy, who rode with us from Delhi
to the god-of-the-Ganges and beyond.
*Scholarship and poetry, I'm told.
Well, one of the two gods you serve
understands the difference between past
and present*, his breathing turning sharp
as we approached, and he stroked his thighs

again and again. *The Ganges
is India's creation story. I would like to stop,
if we could, to drink the water*

Canto 8

The distance not far. Good-looking Ari
in his second residency in pediatrics
caught a ride with us
from Geneva to Lyon and asked to sit
in the back with our three little ones.
He knew his parents from a time-chewed
picture he showed the children
crowding his elbows. Orphan
of time and place, the only one left
because of Birkenau

I started life late. His smile . . .

Canto 9

Solitude of home in a distant country:
the long-torsoed Indian in the Delhi airport
beside a Star-of-David-emblazoned bulge
of suitcase. "When did you decamp
from Israel?" *Twenty-six hundred years ago,
my friend. They say we lost ourselves
when we lost our luggage,
but there's no old home, only home*
or the long way home or homelessness

Canto 10

Morning screek that came as refugee ragman,
horse and wooden sledge careening fitfully
yet surely over uneven fractures

of old avenues. How long does it take
to begin as a stranger in Montreal
and end knowing this each seventh day
when he reads the Yiddish weekly
in Mile End? He survived,
had lives, and spoke words softly
to his horse as if from one of those lives,
from deep inside of it.
On Mondays he cracked his whip
on the winter's breath to close gaps
of the day's disrepairs

Canto 11

Although "the past is never dead" may be
Faulkner's fugitive wisdom, the past
and its dead rescue little, not even
a bankrupt Black Sea archeological mission,
its two hundred years of "exemplary service."
And career spies into what once was,
regardless of the distance, know that
with the past and its dead the costs of one
depends on more than the other

Canto 12

Even then the dead of Assos, Turkey,
seemed strangely out of place, the way
time often is, but they would be changed
in a moment the apostle, as always,
told those stopping to listen;
everyone would be transformed with them,
no matter how great their number,
and perhaps before that day
flashes into view he might return

But now he had to pack his tent
and with his footman walk it down
far below on the road that cordoned
the broad bias of the necropolis,
down to the boatman as the sun heaved up
out of the Aegean black, turning it blue

The bargaining briefer than the dawn,
the hollow-faced helmsman, anxious
to push off for home on the almost visible
Macedonian shore, run with the wind
to his port next to the city's new agora
and the pavestone street rising to the theatre
wrapped round in the marble's godlike light

There are sudden shudders of change
that worn-away centuries,
tired of themselves and their forgetfulness
about almost everything, leave alone
because they cannot stop anything
on their own: first a shiver-dance
of marbled inscriptions
as sarcophagi rocked in place, then
a loud earth-groan, the air angry as a fist
and the slope a thunderous runaway herd
lurching down as one with the sweetbriar
toward the derelict Greco-Roman road below,
a mass migration of the Assos dead
startled by something higher up
and more recent or older than them,
by this breakaway of what had been
(time-wracked seers said
the new church built with cornerstones
that had shouldered Athena's wishes
on the highest part of the acropolis),
the priests' and limestone flesh-eaters'

work left unfinished, some sarcophagi
stopped by the large leeways
in the roadbed rocks.
The water's restlessness casts off
the newly excavated road.
An unattended tiller hitches nervously
in the lapse of time

Canto 13

Leave the lira-buzzing market
and the long-distance call behind
on the sycamore slope in Amasra,
and step through shallows to a laddered rock
to stare out northward over the Black Sea
to your grandfather's Crimea.
His father's grave. An hour later
only long-suffering distance finding itself
alone without the green contours
of the *there* and *then* given time to be

Canto 14

When time nodded and sat quietly down
beside me beneath the flowering chestnut
in Hamburg's Alster Park,
the bench rocked slightly with the day's
unevenness. Sun and slender shadows
sensibly dressed the women
and overdressed the men walking large dogs
on short leashes, not for the sake of the dogs
but for the second soul
of what might be: friend, lover, home.
Time watched as closely as I; we looked
at each other, my silk-smooth valise
and unfinished narrative between us

III. What Comes After

Canto 15

The memory of you this unspoken morning,
Allen Ginsberg, how on the undergraduate green
in the shade of ancient firs your minimal accordion
pressed out harmonium hums
and a litany of eye-watered Oms.
Then, so close, in and out of time,
from your "Kaddish"
Dreaming back thru life. Your time—and mine
accelerating toward Apocalypse,
the final moment—the flower burning in the Day—
            and what comes after,
looking back on the mind itself . . .
and I looking back on Coast Guard ropes
trailing water and Keith's travel-bag body,
his eyes, like yours, wide open

Final moments continue their talkathons
of redemption and disaster
as did the lone blackbird in the firs
endlessly talking back to you as though
to let us know the moment is still here,
that there is more to say
even as time laps our lives

There is more to say on what comes after

Canto 16

They said if Trotsky could remain faithful
there would be time enough

Russia might heed the unburied,

give them names, make this a choice

They said if Stalin could only remember
one repetition in his seminary chants

They said if the faithful cast votes
for eternity, the earth won't wait

to turn cold, and so they dressed
in layer upon layer of separateness

and fled. The head-high rosewood
pendulum clock and its counting loud as keys

in a prison door were left with neighbours
who stayed, who didn't believe every alarm

would reinvent the vanishing point
of staying behind. It took thousands of miles

to resettle prayers and promises adjusted
like the hands of silver-plated pocket watches

to the failures learned, and it took a lifetime
to stop winding those watches

despite a clock in every room

Canto 17

Shrivelled prison camp letters
on the white table. Words, only a few,
pencilled in the cramped left margin
of the page, and of the next letter,
characters minuscule,
half-formed, almost horizontal

gathered like hurried ellipses,
the indecipherable interrupting
an off-white quiet
with a disordered feeling of time.
Here and there the start of a flourish
distracting the eye from finding out
how much graphite has vanished,
how many the spaces where the pencil
tip left a scar

Even if you could make out the names
as you hold the page to the light,
what difference would that make?
but you've let them change
everything else on the page
with a pain much older
than you, a pain that breathes prayers
like unaccountable gaps waiting
for something to follow, no matter
the lost words

Canto 18

West of Winnipeg a scarecrow falls,
the garden leans, summer is over.
And Ashbery's "The Skaters":
How much
of any one of us
survives?

Canto 19

And yet you're pondering the road ahead,
eager to drive on although part of you delays,
not a plea-bargaining, but a bargaining
nonetheless, the windshield breathing chill

into whatever still has interest
other than the endless float of plains
after crossing the 49th into the deep dark
of Montana an hour before dawn,
the headlights' twin tangents
searching the highway . . . nothing but
Montana and Montana and a star
showing its off-and-on faintly through
as though being there is almost enough,
breathing measured by the tick-tick-tick
of the turn signal that has regulated
mile after mile of the oncoming
and the mirrors' obscurities

Canto 20

Morning crosswinds drawing out
memories, their swerves along for the ride:
did Ari finally make his home
somewhere? just what did Agniezska mean
by "the Polish question"? why
are the world's pilgrims at war
with themselves? why do brochures
gloss Mile End as the future, an afterlife
of sorts? The stream alongside broad
and deep like the sky, as if ready
for what's coming, broken blue
of the Rockies now and then appearing
as far as before, the long before anchored
by distance and time as a mountain is

Canto 21

Broad-shouldered and shoulderless roads
seeking out more than a pilgrimage
to a planned arrival, although the car radio

wavers in and out with moral cheer,
the road less smooth as it seeks
the rest of this day, next storefront town.
Pauses, perhaps too many, and fewer hawks
roosting like sentinels in treetops
after you turn toward the blue sawtooth
of glacial peaks into the western edition of sky
and deep mountain valleys. The car
labours hard across the cordillera,
a mixed blessing that forgets itself
on the other side in the changing light,
and you take comfort in keeping going.
Some of the clouds have gnawed into
the evening's glare, some transfer light
into dark, some have been left far behind,
the sky-drift scattering itself like clothes
in an open field as you stare the miles down.
You will arrive late

Afterword

Always the astonishment of distance
and the days, welcome or not.
The sky's millennia seeking out progress
from the past's torn fold-lines, the sun
refusing to grow smaller,
time still drawing to itself
the horizon's red edge
as roads become familiar,
as the distance ahead grows into
a darkening guest room
for the day's end to become word,
word become prophecy

headwind shudders pushing back

FIGURAL MOMENTS

"Existence reveals reality
when the flux discloses something that
dominates it"

~ George Santayana,
The Life of Reason, Volume 1, Chapter 5

28

Life Stories

Child prodigy despite a violin too large.
First in class despite trances that twisted you
far into yourself. Taking in
languages, philosophy, religions,
astrophysics and so on, that too
was you: everything too easy.
And bartering sleep for all-night memoirs.
The unexplored veins of life stories,
their far corners of surprises,
kept you awake, and the dark retreated
in favour of secrecy

At first you didn't recognize how large
an opening chapter can be, and the second
even larger. Later there was much to learn:
why a linguist like you should oppose
grammars of hell, even the least theoretical,
how to forget, how to sleep again at night,
how to turn silent on your violin,
which experts said was of considerable value,
the reasons for selling it to a dealer
instead of passing it on to your son
or to friends who used to come over
on Sundays to play Mozart and Mendelssohn
with you in the grape arbour or great room

The time you questioned me about
your second chapter I sensed a modesty
you didn't have, although I wanted to ask
if you might risk adding at least one more
chapter – perhaps about everyday
assaults on happiness, starting with
what the gang of Russian soldiers did
to your mother

But for that, you would have had to lock
your office, I suspect,
like someone with secret files, find
the right key, let the evidence speak for itself,
drop your habit of slight flourishes at
the beginning and end of words and ignore
misspellings, let the script grow smaller,
more compact, the ink bleeding through
wherever you stopped longer than usual,
like trying to find
a tighter line, take it home

I can only believe you will have figured out
how much of your folio notebook
you'd leave empty, reserved for increments
your prayers had ignored,
the many unplanned departures,
where you were starting this time,
how much you'd take along,
if anything was wrong. If you should allow
the old yearning to return.
No doubt you would have fingered
those empty pages more than once,
counted leaves to the end

like words held back as I write
your memoir, more and more certain
than I was that you are there
vowing greater silence this time
and more erasure, thinking the unimaginable,
the revolution you always said you feared,
the refugees, how they lost
their children, how they lost everything except
memories of a few melodies
and missing friends, the shouts, the alarms

I left much of this unmentioned,
a courtesy to the editor I met
last week at his invitation.
A single volume, many brief
and lively chapters, he advised.
I stalled for time, for the right words,
not argument, agreement or that flash
of silence before his words or mine
moved on – I wanted to point you out,
introduce you by name, explain
that you too lived elsewhere.
Tell you of old friends who have died

Litany for Alice Munro

That promises form walls of light
in snow-blind air

That desire is caught between itself
and an unturned page

That the dreams of a young woman shall be twisted
and twisted like wire

That ignorance will laugh at one
as well as at many

That the smile of a neighbour at your door
is not without meaning

That confession in stories is comfortless;
they are unforgiving

All She Wanted Was to Move to the City

If you returned, Mother, from the east
for part of a morning or the west
for the evening, surprised us
with your everyday clothes,
it wouldn't be to startle anyone,
all of us older, nor to be young
once again, to live in others' lives,
their sudden joys and jealousies,
the swift change of mind, the little left
unsaid

       and it wouldn't be
to speak of others or yourself
or the day's long commands of work,
evening peaceful, the lamp lighting
the corner table and single chair
in the room you called your own,
a book open face down,
two apple cores brown
on a small white plate

In a hamlet of belonging
everything belongs somewhere
although shadows struggle to escape.
A step or two ahead your shadow
feels the village coming,
holds its breath as you feel time's
swerve again to the other side.
Away from where we are

Latest Economic Theories

The foyer's midday TV screen
ruminates on summaries and statistics,
on how to take them in.
A friend on the fourth floor, Ward G,
a stickler for the world's economic fits
of fever or fatigue will be watching,
she who won't let economic frailty
or the unceremonious accuracies
of her own decline dismiss the poor,
and who never read a World Bank report without
*it needs a truer editor. The future
shouldn't be given to subtleties*

nor to nervous pressures of the now,
like the day she turned a hospital-reference white
and passed out when told to lie back as the nurse
reached through a clumsy resignation
of tubing to hook the shrunken bag of blood
higher. When my friend came-to she
wanted to know could I stay another hour
or two to help sort an untogetherness
of stapled and loose pages in order to start
getting ready for next week's exam
on the latest economic theories.
She knew the dangers of surmise
going off on its own like a patient
through the main entrance into the rain
without a discharge. The alarm.
She would be more careful,
her shunted arm really not hurting
much, and outside the window
when we looked that way
tracks of small cloud bruises in the sky
promising better weather

The Farm Was for Tax Purposes

All three were moving, he leaping
from the tractor and then ahead
of both tractor and mare.
If a pasture is really that slippery
the earth may defer, give way for a body
in the exact shape of that body
for the time it takes the tractor to grow
monstrously over him and move on
to growl and snap into the gate post.
Because earth and body have become one,
the earth will scream as he frees himself
from its embrace and drags his body
with him claw-like past the tractor
and through the open gate, the Arabian
gone, and the lapse of time from the gate
to the garage to the car and the car's horn
to his wife's wordless shriek
will be longer than any news report

on how to extend one's life
by fifteen years or more by simply
paying attention and following advertised
guidelines, even if he won't keep
rules ramrod straight although rods
have become half his spine, even if his days
release themselves in single file
with hit and miss of controlled substances,
even if he has outlived his wife

and today dismantled the gate's hinges
and let it fall on its own, a kind of separation,
although it fell against him
as he leaned into it a day after
he had ridden the badly dented tractor

with new backhoe red as
an October briefing.
A neighbour's two sons alongside:
the possibility of order and action
to manage an afternoon's compactness
at the softest part of the pasture,
to help him bury the mare
complete with bit and blanket, her eyes
still fixed forward. His silence,
like the boys', waiting for something
no longer apparent, that something more

The Dutch Immigrant's Daughter

A hard inwardness except for the room's
window in the middle
where the day starts with a tree's
leathered dark at the left margin
and a tenuous withdrawing
toward pale green
that narrows the garden corridor.
Farther back the deeper green
of fields sloughing to the right margin
and its moment of red, a cow looking
beyond the painting –
a scene for old Dutch masters

She wonders whether her parents' first home
looked like this, or is it the wrong desire
familiar in its comfort, its fading.
She really should begin another piece,
more daring this time, perhaps
a breakthrough in plane her part-time
tutor might say, or perspective inferred
from bold colour-shapings that go
back and forth and come closer
yet stay where they are, brush strokes
loaded up but less even, seeking surety.
She wonders if this is what redeemed
Van Gogh's seedtime and the brevity
of his missionary posting, which she
has read about, his hope of helping out
the god of transformation
by giving away what he was,
which is why he would have overlayered
the house and room and field
on her easel again and again
until the greens were transmuted

into the true presence and full force
of blue and the paler greens
into a tumult of yellow

New want stretching an imprecision
of nerves, something like promise
spending its unaccompanied time
on the other easel, on its sheer space,
and a palette of eyes that watch brushes
in place, nothing loaded.
So much to make new,
and the day already emptying itself

Emmanuel Lévinás and the Unconditional

So, far less than unconditional respect
for the physicians, for the trifling over
how to count days caught up
in the middle of concerns,
Heidegger, for one – he was wrong,
but how much may never be settled

For all that, what's right is still a house
where you have memorized ceiling, wall
and open door, where words come and go
like muted radiance of the plum tree,
the leaves' confusion almost praise,
a welcome like faith's embarrassment
or hunger holding on
now that you're home again, able to read,
and there's something to work against
and for. Where the sun concentrates
whatever it touches, the horizon, the tree

plums purpling in the day's ripe hours
dusted by air like that feeling for friends,
the warmth throughout down to fingertips.
Your wife strokes the plums,
presses them with both hands, steps
back. Tomorrow, perhaps

No rash promises you made when you returned
from Ukraine. No painful privacy of pleas,
and your words for others will not refuse
the patience of twisting free of you.
Some of these words you've already
written down, and most of them are sure
you'll get there, but not on your own.
Time's quiet urgency

and the flagstone path to the plum tree
wait to help like vessels of your life
that want to teach a closed one how
to open again
but instead open themselves more

You remember the time you bent low
to leave the tree, how a large bough
brushed your hair. That infinite deference

Hymnal with Pressed Flowers

Father's chest alive
against the boy's cheek like the half-size
cello's strings and belly when the bow
was straight and true, gravitas of cadences,
ardour of voices singing as one,
and a church window's
frosted band of morning light.
At the boy's feet two book-pressed
flowers separated from their blueness,
one of them come apart
inside a lacquered rainbow's shimmering

***

He needed to return
and be surprised by how the closet
music study shuns the house,
how he needs to pull the blind up
carefully as his father used to do
to stop its backsliding,
open the narrow window just enough
for containment
and sum up what's housed here,
a randomness only his father
could have explained,
farrago of sheet music, scores,
jaded covers of music history,
theory, harmony, a photo album
of a boy's years in Russia,
siblings who died young.
The order here is eyes
and fingers, his father's shortcut
to knowing for the moment,
for a lifetime

Nearest the window
the hymnal by itself, dried flowers
behind the spine torn at the top
and flakes of desiccated light
drifting down as he lifts the hymnal
to open to the index.
On the back flyleaf
the vague stain of petals and a pen's
broad script that had leached
all the way through at the time:
> *So many reasons for the heart's pain,*
> *For all that's old*
> *And cannot heal.*
> *But if you were to become its meaning,*
> *It will be like hymns you can't forget.*
> *It will not leave without you*

Fingers press the page
like silence prolonging
the last note beyond its sound –
There are gods who sing
to those they wish to destroy,
but why these words
at the end of a book of hymns?

Walking as If

Even walkers will confuse impression
with being impressed.
You've always felt impression means
difference and being impressed takes time
and distance. That may be your reason
for walking hunched onwards
a step or two ahead of yesterday
like refugee men of Yarrow
with their wives, the woman reaching
forward as if to touch the man's sleeve
when it swings back from the rest of him
and his day-break direction

which is also yours, following, visor down
just below morning blindness,
eyes still too full of light,
and you realize for the first time,
it's the sun's many days that tease
resinous breath from the dark stand
of grand firs you passed an hour ago
when you set out walking into the universe

The man shambles to a stop
and starts anew, he and she
on either side of the sun. Song sparrow,
more than one, colonizing shadows
beyond the broken field,
small shivers in the foliage
there, again, on both sides, but where exactly,
and the man is stuck once more
in a backward moment of turning
as if to let you know
these figural moments belong
to anyone

THE MORTAL:
IMAGES AND MEMORIES

"And send imagination forth
Under the day's declining beam, and call
Images and memories . . .
For I would ask a question of them all"

~ W.B. Yeats, "The Tower"

In Response to Questions

According to Kassim Ali you are half yourself;
the other part is questions between
you and others. Not only questions
that fold into a single idea about themselves
like your place of birth or whether God
is less glorified by what's imagined
than by what has been or surely will be

but also whether a mountain road
is most real just before it vanishes,
whether the dead break away like a flock
of swallows startled toward eternity,
whether answers far off
can trust a memory of miles
and their markers to find you

or how to read the first clear day
of your spindly years and Anne's early fullness,
why she asked to sit beside you
on the high school bus, how
your moving over was like the miracle
of translation, words missing, yet the fields
and sky beyond saying yes

why she said yes to your LPs of Vivaldi
and Mozart, their dreamy, joyous continuos
in close embrace, their cries from the depths,
and you dreamed defiance
until she returned ruined records
from a year of non-stop bad needles,
what was left like the sound of dry spear
grass snapping in the wind, and she said No
to your question of why, after every ride,
she asked to walk the last quarter mile

home. And if one day your questions
become the person you thought she was,
you will let her breath grow calm and warm
among them, a steady rhythm
like her small facial tics, free of terror
or desperation, and not that moment
twisted at the centre by the steering
wheel and dashboard, how it lost its hold
on the body and both of her shoes,
the question still pleading in her eyes

Housekeeping

Because no one's ever been properly buried
our neighbour has ruled out a funeral
and assigned every part of himself
to his yard, equal dust of ash, if possible,
under each tree in the garden
right next to our lives,
biographies and histories to his wife,
a box of poetry books to me, a few spines
wrinkled but no edge torn, not a page corner
folded down of poems he has memorized
like the exactness
with which he quotes Shakespeare
Remember
First to possess his books; for without them
He's but a sot as I am

He says the black yarmulke of the catbird
beating wings giddy in the granite bath
is as beautiful as the finch's gold
in the cone flower. And would I be
neighbourly enough to dig up
the derelict cotoneaster by the front door?

I return books I've pulled
and leave the box with my name
for another time, step with him over
hand drill, hammer, screws, hinges
and closing tube at the door.
He's replacing the screen-door himself,
a bad fit from the time he hung it,
removed it this morning
after it slammed all night
in a wind the weather forecaster
had missed

Some problems new,
dying, for instance, his caged lamp
no longer absorbing the dark
under floorboards, in nooks,
in moisture-blackened basements,
in the attic, searching out mistakes
missed last time

He'd just as soon keep his books,
every one of them, and whatever else
is left, wrongs and their offer of truce,
even that which worked out fine
or never needed his attention,
his mouth a half frown of a traveller
with that far look for someone other than me
come to meet him, and yesterday
he read in a natural history magazine
how the dusky gopher frog
when held up to broad daylight,
covers its eyes with its hands

Alzheimer's Resource Finder

We lock the room, watch the mind
go missing like his baton,
scrapbook, marriage photo.
He sorts one by one what was taken along
to this room of small echoes: a hymn
that promises a balm in Gilead, a map
of the other side of town where he used to live,
the picture of a mother he never knew,
full face with the corners torn,
name of the river that salmon have forgotten
for years, the Russian Jew's simple poem
about a good life as affliction that someone
set to music pitched for a mid-range
of losses and the painful privacy
of an all-day earworm hum,
permission to know the words or us
gone amiss like an afternoon disturbed

We agree with the doctor. We're family,
and families don't get exactly what they expect.
Sometimes more, a past, for instance,
with its rescued years and regrets
entire as the horizon beyond
the bay, and the times he sang arias
with Samuel Ramey. Sometimes less,
partial scores that don't belong together,
the homelessness of a soiled vest,
eyes emptied by all that's unavailable,
abandoned, fog up from the bay, tree
by tree banishing whatever was there,
even the garden he stared at moments ago
through the window where a Norway rat
looked for seeds in the broken
bird feeder

Addendum Filed with the Medical History

The chair was too far from the telephone
and your hearing aids off; that's why your hip
shattered without a sound, you said,
startled by all those wheelchairs in the foyer
gathered in gossipy, desolate queues
but not by the death of your few remaining friends
or the sudden coming on
of blindness, the nakedness of your white stick.
You agreed with your sister's *too often
there's hell to pay between points A and B*,
the sister who had helped you give up on hell,
a space too large for anyone's need
or bequest and laid out entirely
in a single pattern like a city
when night swallows street corners whole

The right hemisphere's first hemorrhage
rearranged its loyalties on what to keep
and what to let go. Why regret certainties
your husband salvaged from ancestral wreckage
and left for you as a tidy inheritance?
Why cherish grievances instead of a reading
machine, or your new immigrant friend
who painted the colours of her veneration
and with simplest words helped you see
how they worked together?
Her voice is a kind of seeing: your chin
over your dinner tray as you wiped your mouth
with the back of your good hand,
a tribute to fine flavour and God's refusal
to confiscate small pleasures or curiosities
insubordinate as your epidemiologic theory
of the chapel's singing groups

But another bleed can eat its way
like miles of fire before the chill sets in
and leaches the need to hold years and place
together, a fading landscape of memory
with a thin clear stream still seeping through
a bog, small recognitions bubbling
like dark water of winter under sunlit ice.
And you listened for the wheelchaired painter,
who couldn't remember the brush strokes
of rehab or you, mere detail
unthreatening as a stranger far off
in the parking lot
or gravelly spatter of the sprinkler against
your hospice window. You slowly threading
the room's emptiness with your hand

Grace Holding Its Breath

When a father disowns his son
a door and new double lock become
necessary, time and place matter,
and when the son leaps
into the night sky shimmering below,
a bridge is necessary, and a Bible
open to the twenty-second Psalm.
And it's necessary
to say he died unexpectedly

After the readings
there's a moment that travels
timeline's sleepless shadow
with the final measure
of "Amazing Grace," left hand
whispering to the fingerboard's
far end, the guitar stilled
yet somehow remembering
the plectrum's last note
from that moment ago,
grace holding its breath,
holding

farther and farther away

Real-time News
For Bob Simon, in Memoriam

People find pleasure in caged parrots
and trust their wisdom of repetition
you said to my wife at dinner in Istanbul

and you answered no
when the waiter repeated his question,
choosing instead a red olive
to hold inside your cheek like a pause.
We were discussing Ukrainian farmers
who satisfied Stalin's gluttonous plan
with five years of eating their seed
grain as well as their children dying
of hunger or already dead,
a large reckoning in a large land.
Mother Russia knew because
journalists had learned to move eyes
without moving their bodies
and speak without moving their lips,
something not taught today
in Journalism school

In our kind of work
we don't wash our hair every day
and acquaintances are everywhere
but friends few. Nothing is sure

When I mentioned Murrow you let the ghostly
great ones walk past,
leave us alone, most of them strangers
long before their final farewell.
The ache of acquaintance that didn't go away,
how it's still there with breaking news

and no one ready to explain
how a body leaves silvered years,
the stretch of another long day's work
and a frown of diligence behind
in the rear seat of a mangled black
limousine, or why friendship
does not deserve death,
and in this world of much acquaintance,
death does not deserve a friend

The Mystery of Clarity; the Clarity of Mystery

*Poets today tend to be clearer – sometimes
all too clear.* Stanley Kunitz

My uncle's cows will have died one by one,
cows don't live that long, a few
staying on whether or not he had plans
he wouldn't have time to use, or whether
there was anything left to plan for,
whether he had missed anything –
that morning's first harelip glares
between Idaho conifers,
the sudden curve, the Greyhound bus . . .
Stillness, everything withdrawn

everything. There are times when plans
can't do a thing, not even begin to announce
themselves like my uncle's tenor voice
on the telephone, frantic to speak from his dairy
on the weather's behalf, blizzard
of the century that closed our valley
with a week-long apparition
from the sky downward.
I fastened the word unlucky under my chin,
guessed road and drainage canal
along its side and lurched against failure
through paroxysms of wind that buried my scarf
under crests of drifts remaking themselves
as they raced endlessly like clouds
to pass themselves, to catch up

When you're helping your cousin and uncle
dig out the farmhouse porch
and trench a path across the yard,
beyond footprints already vanished,

to the barn's double door,
human faces as well as cows have
that tangible distance of unfamiliarity
that doesn't go away as you feed
Holstein milkers staring straight ahead,
noses running and steaming against the cold
within, several stumbling and one
falling for a moment against her neighbour's
white and black as we watered them
nose and mouth in a pail because
the water-bowl intakes were frozen

Outside, we poured large cans of warm milk
into the storm's pallid light and white pursuit
as my uncle stared back into the barn,
as though the mystery of what doesn't end
may have changed the odds
and knowing them needs guidance
far beyond the fury of digging
head-high paths to the barn to save cows,
his eyes steadily clearing something away
as he heaved the doors shut

What he intended or didn't want
may be as unclear years later
as any moment of fear without assurance,
or as complications of the heart still trying
to sort things out long after the fact,
or as accounts beyond self-help
from now for what was then,
or as words charged with this secret life,
something like my uncle's
Fortunate – so far

A Matter of the Heart

The main business of time is guarantees,
but the small print lists warnings −
ask the jogger almost well enough
to restart an early morning

or ask God or the heart
how surety can go missing
like a surgeon's lost sponge found inside
the hard-wired ribcage reopened
and closed again, the breathing
unafraid of itself, its urgency
not telling us either way, but "much deeper
than before" my brother says,
his hand searching the fingerboard
frets of scars over the heart's quiet joy,
his words like nerves
to their smallest ends
seeking what is still there

and he shuffling closer
to watch with me in closed caption
the journalist's year-end list
of immortal ones who died
despite precise wording of praise
that has stalked them

to watch the captions correct themselves
and say again what they've learned
about immortals and us

On Her Birthday

Time's on-edge abrasions
have chafed us but not fingers
in one another's palms, the shoulder
stroke, this life-long gift of touch
that doesn't have to guess the axis
of our waking hours or watch by degrees
our balance as we step atilt
past tinnitus to worktable and chair

These small repetitions of love,
more than handrail assurance of stairs
or the blue shine of hiking sticks
at the door where morning still
wants in, wants out,
and none of the birds
on the orchard slope are frightened
by your comeliness on the path

THE PURPOSE OF TRAVEL

"The question is not where did the traveller go?
What places did he see?
It would be difficult to choose between places—
But who was the traveller?
How did he travel?"

~ H.D. Thoreau, *Journal Volume 4,*
January 11, 1852

Find What Isn't Missing
To the memory of Jim Berlin

They say there's a hum in everything,
a universe getting ready, and quite unlike
the rag collector's morning shouts
below our balcony in Kolkata,
the student march in Seoul,
a street evangelist's alarms in London,
a pregnant beggar's call in Budapest
to her cohort across the street,
night-cap screams of the church elder
at his newest wife in the flat below
in Midland, Texas, cacophony of crows
escorting the black and white
of a nest-robbing eagle across the clear-cut
on the Harrison River trail,
a straight-line raucousness fading into the west

Jet-lag sleep, the hum of waking
that takes its place, daybreak simple as feet
touching the floor and a rat-a-tat outside
the window, emptying itself of repetition:
the dead walnut tree's grey nakedness
found by the sun and commandeered
by the red and black of the woodpecker's
walk up the tree's spine

Nowhere but here, the journal notebook open
on the night table, yesterday's in-flight entry

the purpose of travel:
adapt consciousness to world

the purpose of writing on travel:
adapt world to words

the purpose of reading on travel:
adapt consciousness to words

the purpose of travelling without a list
of what you've lost:
find what isn't missing . . .

My wife's bare shoulders and teal housecoat
shrugging off the chill, our Boston terrier
shivering at the door in his deep sleep
nose against corkscrew tail, a trio
of neighbours jogging through their breath,
Jim in the lead, explaining with his hands,
and then their absence, patience settling in

I pour my wife an over-full cup of coffee
and ask whether we're done with travelling
this year. "One suitcase will have to be replaced."
A question of readiness

                  Like Jim,
for years first one up for the family trip,
dressing in the dark, loading his car
in white-stocking feet,
legs and arms nervous with intention
because he knew wife and sons were about to dress
and he would soon have packed as much as needed,
maps stuffed into the passenger-side pocket
because he had memorized roads in advance,
all of them important, like starting over

The time we mused our new car
from the Montreal pier to the Pacific,
the sun rose behind us,
and berserk flies escaped through the chill
of the car's cracked window. Each day

cross winds on the wheel eased off
and plains unfolded their calm horizon by
horizon. Once home we unpacked our cargo –
first the disappointments, then suitcases, cartons,
fatigue. We fell asleep without undressing

But Jim, you would unpack your car,
find your jogging shoes and run for an hour,
the usual route. That's how they found you

There's a formlessness within us all,
incomprehensible, out of the pale,
and lying close together will not help.
No faint-edged sky to hold the mind,
what can be done poised against nothing-at-all

And there's bereftness, even in counting steps
to the basement to inspect our children's
numbered cartons taped more than once
for a move, turn each on its side to the window
to see if time has bled its grey through
the bottom, if the scrawl on the largest box
is legible, the children far from what
they left behind, and they may have taken
too little with them of what they need

A small start of mildew, but only
on the tallest box heavily taped,
its sides slack when boxes next to it
are moved away. One day I'll open that box,
a morning when we're not going anywhere.
The silver knife a man in Cold-War Prague
traded for a copy of *The Atlantic*
will cut the tape cleanly and the box will open
almost by itself as though time and place
are still the same as cities where our children

once stood shoulder to shoulder among
other children with what one day
would seem apocryphal, forgotten by them all

The box was much too large to start with
considering what goes missing over time,
but it's the emptiness I fear, contents
removed several at a time, unrecorded
inventories, nothing to be repacked
or sent on, and in the end the top
freshly taped again out of habit,
as if to regulate what's left inside.
The only name on the box crossed through
by one of the children,
someone who's figured out the more a box
is emptied the more is missing,
and only the emptiness belongs to us

Jim, you would have said *check it out,*
most things can be used and some
are still there and should be taken along.
I imagine you, sweat-laced from the run,
bending down to grasp this box sagging
into itself, lifting it carefully
with both arms, not tightly, moving it
closer to the light
to find what isn't missing

Homecoming

Rainbow rooster tails, silence
of colour shedding itself everywhere
in the sea's aftermath of light:
whale spouts that hold you
and your wife at the deck-rail's white
despite three calls for dinner
as you sail through the Gulf
of St. Lawrence, coming home,
hunger's expectations gone
with the first vague shimmer of land.
You want to stay here,
at sea on the promenade deck,
to watch each iridescence find that moment
where it's sheared off in thin air, vanishes,
but the image remains

When the ship blurted its full-throat groans
and left the Rotterdam shipping lanes behind
as afterthoughts, a woman in underwear
rose from her deck chair
and leaned on the rail –
no more Russkie – stepped backwards,
reached down hand over hand behind her
to find her dress as the brass ensemble
broke out a waltz on the deck below

A monstrous blue shadow defines outline
and depth in sliding by, flukes almost at rest,
toward the Atlantic like a wistfulness
that has you following,
and you know if you returned
it would no longer be as a guest
uninvited by a year or more
on the Continent with vacations in Cornwall

and the Lake Country. Suddenly,
I know you didn't want to leave;
forgive me for voting the way I did,
but I think it's right for both of us —
the breeze stiffening my wife's hair,
the air changing as a door is closed;
behind us diners in formal dress
strolling by, the sea silvering,
the way we've come turning black

Covent Garden

Attention thrust like an immigrant
into the public sweat of anonymity,
disorder of bodies, and a raw gargle of sounds
you want to agree with despite jet-lag
catatonia, the threat of evening rain,
and a cue across the street. Pirouette
of Bahama-white boat shoes,
calf-length trousers black as the high-hitch
of suspenders, and twists
by two chalk faces stutter-juggling
even as longing gives notice next to you:
long-limbed singers, metronomed
arias and duets from *Cosi Fan Tutte*,
the orchestra a finger-fidgeting electric
keyboard almost aced by a pigeon spooked away
by the gritty havoc of a cell-phone
argument behind you. Into the upturned hat
a Drury Lane drunk's largesse, pennies
nameless as your bank withdrawal
in a pocket of the coat your daughter donated
last week to her charity auction,
a matter still to be worked out

The opera house and yawning Transport
Museum may want to offer other streets
and directions from tomorrow or the London
of last time in order to find you
with a Mozart of pure play, mordents and trills
spot-on, less face-up juggling,
body not going wrong as yours, short breath
felt in passersby fashionably dressed
or plain as breakfast porridge and kippers
and lacking any desire to hide
their perfect grace as they look your way

The Procession in Soweto

Mouse-brown face hollowing out cheekbones
and eyes raw as a craving for fullness, a scarecrow
emptiness of sleeves beside you in the shade
of the eucalyptus as marchers grow larger,
both of you forward to see what's coming:
banners riding a long procession through heat waves,
the marchers singing in four-part harmony.
A raised fist out of her sleeve,
the moment sudden as her vanishing
into the alley's dust and double turn behind you
as the lead singers pass, as you are held in place
by what you do not understand

A stirring-up you would have believed in
if only you had been ready,
the narrative gone at its unfolding, lost,
not like what can't be remembered
but something unaccounted for
like a camera cocked without film

You've memorized the melody re-sung even after
the last singer passed and followed the others
into the far-down lot beyond the church,
their makeshift conclusion spreading out.
You still don't know why the marchers came,
why the woman in rags showed her fist and fled

The urgency close as the guide
in the endless slum's chemical air
who spoke softly about government monies
always somehow taking their leave,
how day and night eat their own.
Your photograph of the guide shows him
sitting with you at the cafeteria table

Notes on a Moscow Evening

From a nerve bed too firm
and an almost-nap to a slight knock.
You mince steps to the door,
listen, pull open to a singular nothing
but cold air from somewhere else
passing through. You walk to the window
where the day or what's left of it lives.
A pigeon's pell-mell of wings
leaves the ledge for the Stalinist massif
across the street, a people's architecture
of acquiescence, so many rows
of darkening panes, their smallness told
with blunt definition like the syntax
of bullet holes in Mexico City.
Daylight glooming as streetlamps
ignite, as rondos of traffic lights
change each other but repeat themselves,
as a ramrod reach of construction cranes
measures evening's silhouettes
of scaffolding and fading vinyl shrouds

***

You know that even flawed attention
becomes sounds and sounds become attention
whether hearing aids are turned on or off
as you walk the street at night,
which you will do when the interview
of the milky-eyed professor is done.
Arms folded like a Buddha he tells
the TV host it's time for journalists
to crawl out from under the rubble of what
was said and done because of the times,
to forgive the past and, yes, even

today's mistakes,
unlike those who left or writers
who stayed to brood anxieties
outlasting centuries. "Ours
is the only future Russia will see":
the pause cadenced by the host's hands
as though silence is music, which it may
well be tonight but you still want to answer
for him *doesn't the future, like virtue,*
always take some getting used to?

*****

At yesterday morning's street corners
no green space needed for poets
in unimpeachable bronze astride
broad-hipped pedestals. All day
they carry on one-sided conversations
with their hands, their work still not done
because there are those who tried to write
their way out of Russia in poems simple
and mysterious as a stamped exit visa
or tried to find themselves
in a future mostly memorized
that keeps on returning

Somewhere you have read
there are countries whose real name
nobody knows, not even their best poets –
that yearning, hope beyond hope
in Mandelstam and Akhmatova

*****

The second day's language lesson
louder than the bus: "good morning

how are you pardon me thank you please
yes no" repetitions not ready for sideway
jolts or entrancement possibilities,
yet words rehearsed as if to stake a new day,
its rockings and this city, to your life

Those loudspeaker recitals still whispering
to you in the street noise tonight.
Let them be. You walk by the bench
you've occupied before:
a lump of inwardness wrapped round
by rat-grey rags, the body seeming
not really there. Perhaps you should stop;
you look back from the subway maw –
Starbucks and Burger King ablaze

*****

Night's sweet-sour has followed you
to the river like a subway thief's curiosity.
An hour you've stood here, sight clear,
eyeglasses free of rain, umbrella closed,
ankle throbbing because of unlit
rottenness of steps steep down
to the water whose murky name the city
stole long ago, the Moskva stretching wide
to claim city lights in longer length,
hold their shivering in place
against the current

*****

Moskva. Why do you want to know
how this word gathered itself
centuries ago from free-floating
syllables? It doesn't belong to you

any more than the answer
from yesterday's blue-uniform guide
"This building, sir, Lubyanka,
never housed a prison and there's no wall
once used by firing squads"
although my wife's father said
it's simple prayers colleagues left behind
in the bedlam of guards and iron doors
that he heard most clearly in his cell.
And there's a blue eyeshadow stare
and microphone held like a finger to the lips
that was meant to save you and your wife,
help you find words without corridors
or echoes, words without a past,
words firmly taken care of, almost casual,
form fully itself. Form as content
and alien as a father's memoir
or overnight British passport
wrapped in embassy papers,
exit visa, and subterfuge,
alien as this hour before midnight
far from Canada,
memorizing the river's soundless drift,
how lights stay where they are,
where they have been since you arrived
and touched the mud slightly
with your shoe

You reach behind for the stairs' brokenness

The Future as Artifact
For Agnieszka and Piotr

Conductor's score of Chopin's first piano concerto
acquired last year from anonymity,
a Ghetto map inside the front cover

and a glassed-in photomania of skeletons,
their helter-skelter in the Babi Yar underbrush.
Everyone says, "terrible – terrible"

Stone angels agree, and the museum in Riga
confirms black and white stutter-steps
of the videos – the year, the time it took

The Führer fingering mustache and heart
and raking his hair to the left side.
Stalin forward, rising from his chair

hand on chest. All others stand with him.
You must have heard of these artifacts
the curator whispers as someone stops

behind us. *They came as gifts from elsewhere,
and once here it's as if they came alive,
as if they've known every turn of the way back*

The Outside of Things Inside Konstanz

It has turned cold.
Even if the courtesan's eyes
are emptied of sky and sea
and her towering stone head hides the sun,
her breasts are bared, and the harbour
behind her is open to centuries
of arrivals and departures,
their unremarkable wake
and small gusts off the water
repeating themselves endlessly

If the wind won't leave us alone
but presses hard as the cobblestone
underfoot, if late-year asters in the park
have reddened like embers
and a gust has already swirled away
leaves that just fell,
wine is offered in booths, red wine
heated to a vapourous moment
spiced with summer.
This is how the season always is
we are told by others pushing and queuing,
and who else than we, strangers here
but not to a season's outside of things,
retrace steps to see again the way we've come,
the courtesan's tokening distant now
as the half-hour toll of the Minster
of Our Lady, litany of echoes
amending themselves like revenants

The street narrow with shops that remake
each other, a kind of restatement
that keeps a traveller going. The door
of the stone and mortar house

near the Jan Hus museum is of a yellow burn.
We step inside: two women untangling
heaps of habit beside their spinning wheels
and ravelling them anew without
urgency. Behind them on the whitewashed
wall a rote reissue of the museum's
gilt-edged Hus in the old public square,
Be assured, no harm shall come to you
cruciform stake twice his height,
and he is praying an upsurge of flames
higher than the straw and wood,
higher than his hands and the centre of his chest
as though more than he will be left
behind, perhaps ways of remembering
and forgetting, the circle of onlookers
an agreement of summer hues

Why does repetition admit to being
expected? Because it's time and place,
not theory? And not without harm?
The cathedral tower's irruption
of the hourly clamour re-sounds
farther and farther off
as the wheels chatter the tick-tick-tick
of time, as the women sing to each other
in harmony an old hymn
well practiced like nods without looking
up when we step out the door
abiding what we've just left,
abiding each gust outside
still precise as the last

Photographic Mission to Chalki

We're aft agreeing with the photographer.
The Guns of Navarone
could have been shot at the vaulted gleam
of cliff on the east side
of St. George's Bay,
but the on-location sheerness
was here on the starboard side
five kilometres out of Lindos,
the cliffs' large sleeve of grey
riding the sea but not as long
as the cameras' make-believe back then.
We sail past, heading toward the harbour,
the wind whipping book pages
and trying to gather up
the table's navigational map
held down by a brand-new camera
and the small twitches of its long strap

A choice: three of us into the old city,
and two climbing the trail past tourist-saddled
mules up to the remaindered purpose
of the ancient acropolis: ruin
and spendthrift view. In town
the souvlaki, apple-peel tea (*elma kabuk chai*)
and pebble-floor mosaics excellent,
the street a tenuous channel
surprising us with secrets in hiding.
Change for payments much too small

Day not yet slanting down,
breakaway jogging whistle-breathes us
to our boat. We untie, remove shoes,
and sail to Chalki, the cries of landless birds
following like shuttled measures,

flying off without relief

Even from a distance
evening light accepts
the steep-slopes of Emporio,
the island's harbour village, and tells us
to put shoes back on, but not before
"release the anchor chain, throw lines
to the guy on the pier, step aside,
I'll drop the gangplank."
No known form for following
one another on a teetery gangway.
We step discreetly down
between two lines stern to dock cleats
like an open-arms welcome,
the photographer halting on the pier
to slip the camera strap over her shoulder
and finger-mark direction to a restaurant
near the pier before leaning forward
and pointing out to herself small shadows
scuttling away four metres down

The strong-hipped, leaky-eyed man
we'd never met before
who double-looped our cleat ties
stares at the water's wide mouth of ripples
and the camera anchoring
in sea grass, the strap wavering,
almost down, the man's hand
on the photographer's shoulder:
No more, sorry. No more. Finish

On-location words of an end too casual
to translate beyond memory

On opposite sides of the table we swallow

what we don't want to say.
What was left of the meses taken away,
and the waiter hovering, we still not ready
for what has been served to us today.
A few forks test the milky gleam
of sea bass, touch the sea urchin,
almost knuckle the salad of seaweed
and arugula as ripples widen,
running through the colours of sunset,
darkening them

We are learning to set things aside
in silence intimate as our other selves.
The ripples are everywhere

Returning to Rhodes

If you return to the harbour
to tie up where birds once soared
over the grand Colossus
and through the sun's corona,
sky at a standstill,
the sea a genial lingering
as thought of an eternal city,
and if you walk the old Jewish Quarter
where merchants called on Ottoman,
Latino, Greek, biblical Hebrew
and snippets of the new Italian
to take care of their lives,
you might wonder which gift of tongues,
which words, served them better
with assiduous informers,
or Mussolini's goons,
or summer rail connections to Auschwitz,
or with the popular new idiolect
black on the arm,
names taken away to long trenches
of languages and ashen heaps of words

Sicily Does Not Belong to Italy

The day's first purpose is fog
getting slowly up above the circle of scum
awash near the sea wall, higher
than the horseshoe harbour's white sleekness
of four sailing craft stealing slackness
from a makeshift green of fishing boats.
Morning as maker of comparisons, of separations
as the fog winches itself slowly beyond
the red and gold language of secret houses
and local flags high-set farther back,
rolling itself up right out of the air
to leave the hills' peak-sheer barrenness behind.
Ring of lemon light splitting open,
sun as seen by fog swallowing itself

Gulls squark and nod as if they alone
have slipped away from the night
to toe-hitch streaks of sunlight
broadening the randomness
of black stone olives
in the patio tiles

At the sea wall a man stands up, looks about.
How to make use of this day, this place?
I'm imperfectly dressed,
but the temperature is an almost perfect
centigrado, as warm as Celsius

The waiter has brought green olives,
parsley and dry goat cheese

He meant Sicily
when he said "world"

Mehmet of Milâs, Who Teaches Literature

Grandfather Mehmet always walked slowly,
feet thrown out to the side like Chaplin's clown.
He chose our long family name
from one of our shameless newspapers
after the whole world was talking of moving
to the city, after Father taught him to read
our new alphabet, and after Ankara passed
our two-name law to make the Mehmets
far more than we had been so all of us
could be counted for once, but not twice

Pinocchio belongs to Pisa but his nose
belongs to Grandfather's stories,
a whole body's performance, hands,
shoulders, chin, hazelnutty eyes. He lectures
the universe, knife pendular above
stuffed peppers and yogurt. "We Mehmets
are storybooks that don't grow old."
He looks at me because I'm the only one
listening: "and there are more stories
of Turks like us than there are Mehmets."
Sometimes his words on how our own Mehmets
made room in this world
are fumbled as though the blessed one,
the Prophet, is eavesdropping from shadows
in the next room on his every syllable

Yes, it's a holy name, and it's my name,
same as Grandfather, Father, four uncles
and five cousins. They have that good-looking
Kurdish face. But there are Mehmets
that have a head like old bread soaking
all morning in cold kitchen water,
and not a few are missing two of their four legs,

our neighbour, for instance,
Mehmet the fly-swarming goatherd
in the open field behind us

One of my Uncle Mehmets waits and waits
for his luck to change like old men
fishing off the pier by the No-Fishing sign.
There are Mehmets who do even less
than the ancient gods. Indeed, we Mehmets
are like anthologies compiled
by dubious reasons

But Father
has that red face of a marriage to masonry.
When there is work, he drinks raki
all night and sings songs endless
as our Anatolian plains before cycling
a here-or-there into the sunrise
to build a faux Ottoman mansion
on an old street, or a sugar-cube apartment
like all the others on a new street,
or a boutique hotel with stonework frogs
vomiting into a pool, the plans drafted
by others. He sings to birds that splat
on his unfinished walls and windows.
His hands and feet are the oldest parts of him,
and the pain in his chest is like bad mortar
in a wall built by a charlatan namesake.
When the scaffolding has been dismembered
he can stand almost straight, right there
inside his broken body, and make contentment
a choice. People will know what I mean.
A feeling gleaned from a gaze –

It's something like classroom glances,
despite cell-phone junkies

who give books the go-by, who remind me
of mules trying over and over to eat
their harness, and yet a class
where the Mehmets and others
will sometimes admit to being surprised
how a story page by page can fever the air,
and even if there are more lies in literature
than there are Mehmets, how the story
can hunt for dreamers and first love.
Behind my desk I watch the impatience
of a world dawning between trees of life,
that yearning – a hide-and-seek of the heart.
I let it find them, go home with them,
sleep with its arms warm about them.
No Mehmet or any other name
is like this.

A Journal on Expatriates

No defense for attending your daughter's expat
dinner party, women dismissing
her interior decorating, the swag-bellied
resort manager wangling to seduce your wife,
your words sweet as honey
with dishonesty

***

At the Ortakent restaurant sound of water
lapping the unslaked pier like dogs,
and a fish bone in your throat.
You try to cough, you try to speak,
you toe sand where the long table
touches the sea as if to carry on
where words and white cloth leave off

***

Words shaped by pauses. The widow
who last year buried her husband
here in Turkey and not in Switzerland
speaks with the loudness of the deaf,
syllables naked as her necklace, stepping
one by one into isolation past
her raised glass *what we have in common*
in this beautiful place
are the ways we can be broken

***

Your evening walk the corridor
of sycamores on Neyzen Tevfik Street.
You taste the harbour air, smell

grilled fish, touch a tree's
trunk and think elephants,
camouflage, trees in the Bible.
An outsider, you, but the trees comply
as a yacht multiplies its lights,
unties and growls seaward
on an endless rattle of anchor chain

***

I can wake any time of day
without newspapers from the West,
but the possibilities of being at home
are not infinite here or back
in London; many acquaintances to meet
in my line of work: the epically dressed
green-eyed editor. When you return
to the room's bunches of bodies
leaning into each other, she's in your chair,
drinking your wine

***

His gaze fixed as you enter, as you watch
ant-lines converge between his feet
at the table where he writes a page each day
for his anthology of historical wrongs
that takes Adorno a step farther
without getting up – the highest morality
is not to feel at home anywhere;
his back to the morning, his stare
beyond the sink's helter-skelter of dishes
white as Ezekiel's desiccate valley
or broken Byzantine lath-work
of bones layered like time far down inside
the high hummock, all those centuries

of leached years awaiting resurrection

***

If your sister purchased a house in Antalya
would she spell the word "ex-patriot"?
Would she remember every room
in homes she's lived in, renovations made,
the look of all the lives from which
she's taken leave?

Unlike Father's memoir
for the third time in my life I pioneered
refusing to leave behind secrets kept
with previous homesteads,
taking along attenuated days

***

Denial in Canada is often dressed as wisdom.
It's this that makes us rarely short
of excuses, casting them like bread
on untreated waters,
finding them again in a day
or so, reclaiming what's left,
the heart's inuring game
in a country of expatriates

But pomegranates have begun to bloom
in Lycia, and you are learning the colours
of your awakening.
Schoolchildren dressed in blue and walking
home stop at the orchard gate to ask
your name

The Travel Writer's Benefits Package

After the effort, there are years
and pages that refuse to retire,
but when you do,
words will be your best friends.
They will huddle around you;
they will say to your body *sing*
to your gardens *wait,*
I'll be back and to your lover
should we take only
hand washables?

When once again you come home
years and pages will remind you
that a twelvemonth ago,
and the same time before,
the rain also returned
with a hard-slant edge,
a dark crossing for the words
and you. But this
is where you'd rather be

Author Profile:

Leonard Neufeldt graduated summa cum laude from Waterloo Lutheran University (Wilfred Laurier) and received his MA and Ph.D in the USA. He was appointed Professor of American Studies at Purdue University in 1978. He and his wife have spent most of their professional years in America and abroad, notably in Europe and Turkey. Lecture tours have taken him to India (twice), Germany, Korea and China. "Rootless lives may be as endemic to the Canadian and American West as root-bound ones," he laments, "but in a world of change, there is little defense for either condition."

Neufeldt's scholarly essays and books have been published with Cambridge University Press, Oxford University Press and Princeton University Press, among others. More recently his ninth book of poetry, *Nearness*, was released in 2020 (Silver Bow Publishing). The greater part of this collection could be described as a Northwest and Pacific homecoming. More generally, Neufeldt's poetry considers revolutions, wars, the Holocaust, the power of individual and cultural memory, language as social process, travel and foreign residence as cultural tutorial and, not least, life in and with nature.

www.ingramcontent.com/pod-product-compliance
Lightning Source LLC
Chambersburg PA
CBHW070412200726

48294CB00003B/1170